Ginn Mathematics

TEXTBOOK 2

GINN

Ancient measures.

The Ancient Egyptians and other early civilizations used the lengths of parts of the body as measures.

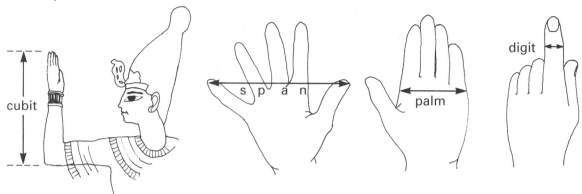

1   The Egyptians took 7 palms to equal 1 cubit.
    Without using a ruler check this

   (a)   for your own span and cubit

   (b)   for those of five friends.

2   Copy and complete

   (a)   … spans are approximately 1 cubit

   (b)   … palms are approximately 1 span

   (c)   Check (a) and (b) for the palms, spans and cubits of five friends.

3   (a)   What is the length of your foot when measured in palms?

   (b)   'The length of a person's foot is between $\frac{3}{5}$ and $\frac{2}{3}$ of the length of his or her cubit.'
         Measure your foot and cubit to the nearest centimetre, then check the statement above. (Remember to take off your shoes!)

4

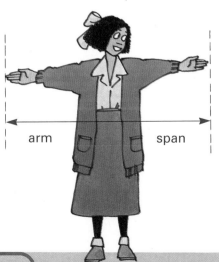

Is your arm span greater than, less than, or approximately equal to, your height?

Thousandths.

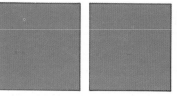

If you divide a hundredth into 10 equal parts, each part is a thousandth.

Units	tenths	hundredths	thousandths
2	8	5	3

2.853

This is read as 'two point eight five three'.

The shaded area in the magnifying glasses below show the number of thousandths.

Write the amounts shown as decimals, as in the example above.

1

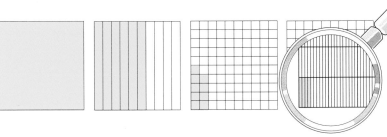

2

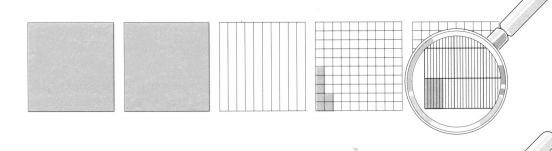

3

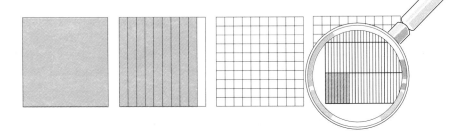

1   Write a decimal to show the number of shaded squares.

(a)

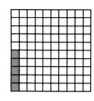

(b)

2   Draw similar diagrams to show these decimals:

(a) **1.89**   (b) **1.57**

3   Give the next three numbers.

(a) 6.5, 6.6, 6.7, __, __, __   (b) 35.07, 35.08, 35.09, __, __, __

(c) 24.7, 24.8, 24.9, __, __, __   (d) 8.03, 8.04, 8.05, __, __, __

(e) 8.098, 8.099, 8.100, __, __, __   (f) 14.096, 14.097, 14.098, __, __, __

4

798.056

Which digit is in the:

(a) tens place?   (b) units place?

(c) hundredths place?   (d) tenths place?

(e) thousandths place?   (f) hundreds place?

Copy each number and place a decimal point so that the statement makes sense.

5

A car travelled from London to Leeds at an average speed of 86594 kilometres per hour.

6

Concorde flies at a maximum speed of 2 179 000 kilometres per hour.

Comparing decimals.

4.0   4.1   4.2

4.00 4.01 4.02 4.03 4.04 4.05 4.06 4.07 4.08 4.09 4.10 4.11 4.12 4.13 4.14 4.15 4.16 4.17 4.18 4.19 4.20

Numbers get smaller.

$4.04 < 4.12$ $4.15 > 4.1$

4.04 is less than 4.12   4.15 is greater than 4.1

Give the number for each letter.

1

2

3

4

Copy and complete these. Put $<$, $=$ or $>$ in the blue circle.

5   3.1 ⬤ 3.4   6   5.9 ⬤ 6.0   7   12.0 ⬤ 12.1

8   4.09 ⬤ 4.10   9   4.00 ⬤ 4.0   10   8.90 ⬤ 8.89

11   3.784 ⬤ 3.782   12   6.29 ⬤ 6.287   13   12.080 ⬤ 12.08

keeping skills sharp

1   Which is greater (a) a pint or a litre?   (b) a pound or a kilogram?
                  (c) a mile or a kilometre?

2   Which of these is nearest to the height of your teacher, A, B or C?

    A 120 cm   B 140 cm   C 160 cm

Rounding.

5.34 is between 5.0 and 6.0. It is nearer to 5.0.
5.34 rounded to the nearest whole number is 5.

Study these examples.

Example 1

12.79 is nearer 13.0 than to 12.0.
12.79 rounded to the nearest whole number is 13.

Example 2

263.52

To round to the nearest whole number,
I just look at the digit in the tenths place.
If it is less than 5, I round down.
If it is 5 or greater, I round up.

263.52 rounded to the nearest whole number is 264.

Example 3

7.615 is exactly halfway between 7.61 and 7.62.
In such cases always round up to the higher number.
7.615 rounded to two places of decimals is 7.62.

1 Round to the nearest whole number.

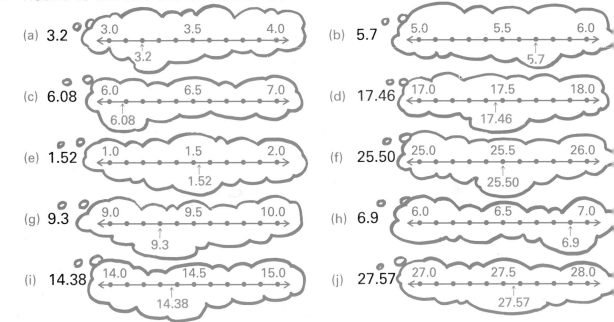

(a) 3.2   3.0   3.5   4.0   3.2

(b) 5.7   5.0   5.5   6.0   5.7

(c) 6.08   6.0   6.5   7.0   6.08

(d) 17.46   17.0   17.5   18.0   17.46

(e) 1.52   1.0   1.5   2.0   1.52

(f) 25.50   25.0   25.5   26.0   25.50

(g) 9.3   9.0   9.5   10.0   9.3

(h) 6.9   6.0   6.5   7.0   6.9

(i) 14.38   14.0   14.5   15.0   14.38

(j) 27.57   27.0   27.5   28.0   27.57

2 Round to one place of decimals.

(a) 8.72   (b) 13.44   (c) 13.43   (d) 13.45   (e) 13.48

(f) 13.49   (g) 13.50   (h) 13.51   (i) 13.58   (j) 13.59

3 Round to one place of decimals.

(a) 49.674   (b) 86.583   (c) 42.486   (d) 128.411

(e) 96.514   (f) 426.883   (g) 2.488   (h) 62.703

4 Round the numbers in question 3 to two places of decimals.

5 Round each price to the nearest pound.

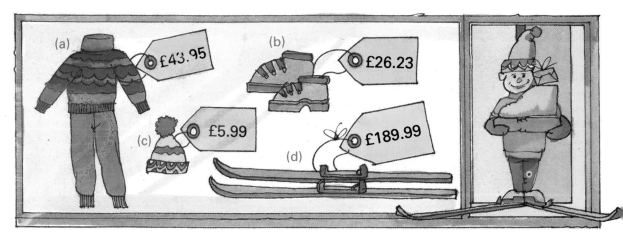

(a) £43.95

(b) £26.23

(c) £5.99

(d) £189.99

Rounding on a calculator.

Mrs Jameson used a calculator to find the cost of 1 packet of juice (£1.33 ÷ 5).

The calculator showed
$$0.266$$

This is £0.266 or 26.6p.
She rounded the cost to the nearest 1p. This is £0.27 or 27p.
On each packet she could save 29p – 26.6p or 2.4p.

The calculations below show the cost in pounds.
Round each (a) to the nearest pound and (b) to the nearest penny.

1 34.6873

2 11.0567

3 99.7145

4 23.1835

5 9.50321

6 18.77777

7 132.67380

8 4.0999999

9 41.30507

10 80.906666

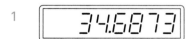

Rounding measures using a calculator.

A runner used a calculator to find her average speed in miles per hour.

The display showed `11.784321`

Rounded to the nearest whole number this is 12 miles per hour (12 mph). Correct to one place of decimals her speed was 11.8 mph.

Both of these are sensible approximations.

1   A motorist calculated the time in hours he would take for a journey:

   It was `1.7534912`

   (a) How many minutes equals 0.1 hours?

   (b) How many minutes does `.7` represent?

   (c) The 5 in the display represents $\frac{5}{100}$ of an hour.
       (i)   Reduce this fraction to its simplest form.
       (ii) How many minutes does the 5 represent?

   (d) How many decimal places would it be sensible to keep?

2   A publisher printed 2000 books at a cost of £5295. Using a calculator find the cost of one book. Round your answer to the nearest penny.

3   The weight of 150 nails is 487 grams. Use a calculator to find the weight of one nail:

   (a)   rounded to the nearest gram

   (b)   rounded to one place of decimals

   (c)   rounded to two places of decimals

   (d)   Which two approximations out of (a), (b) and (c) are the most sensible?

A decimal game.

[ ] is a box in which only one digit must be written.
You are given four digits which must all be used.
You may place a decimal point in any position. (.3670 and 3670. are both allowed.)

For example, use [3] [6] [7] and [0] to make a number between 3.0 and 3.7.

[3] . [6] [0] [7] and [3] . [6] [7] [0] are both solutions, but they are not the only ones.

Find any one solution to each of the following, using the given digits.

1 [0] [9] [1] [4]

(a) The number as near to 9 as possible.
(b) The smallest possible number.
(c) The greatest possible number.
(d) A number between 1.0 and 1.5.

2 [5] [2] [8] [5]

(a) A number between 800 and 840.
(b) The smallest possible number.
(c) The greatest number that is less than 1.
(d) A number between 2 and 3.

3 [1] [3] [7] [0]

(a) The greatest possible number.
(b) A number as near to 72 as possible.
(c) A number between 16 and 18.
(d) A number as near to 13.4 as possible.

4 Make up your own questions but using five digits instead of four.
Play the game with some friends and compare your answers.

Multiplying or dividing decimals by 10, 100 or 1000.

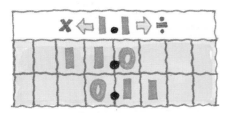

When *multiplying* a decimal by 10, the digits move one place to the *left*.
When *dividing* a decimal by 10, the digits move one place to the *right*.

$3.46 \times 10 = 34.6$ $3.46 \div 10 = 0.346$

Multiplying by 10 makes a number greater, so I must move the digits one place to the left.

Dividing by 10 makes a number smaller, so I must move the digits one place to the right.

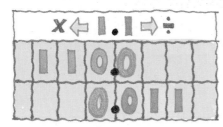

When *multiplying* a decimal by 100, the digits move two places to the *left*.
When *dividing* a decimal by 100, the digits move two places to the *right*.

$829.63 \times 100 = 82\,963.0$
$829.63 \div 100 = 8.2963$

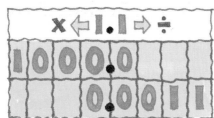

When *multiplying* a decimal by 1000, the digits move three places to the *left*.
When *dividing* a decimal by 1000, the digits move three places to the *right*.

$792.46 \times 1000 = 792\,460.0$
$792.46 \div 1000 = 0.792\,46$

Compare the number of zeros in 10, 100 or 1000 to the number of places you moved the digits in each product or quotient.
Can you find one rule to cover all cases?

Use the rule to find each product or quotient.

1 (a) 5.62 × 10
  (b) 5.62 ÷ 10

2 (a) 83.5 × 100
  (b) 83.5 ÷ 100

3 (a) 9.462 × 1000
  (b) 9.462 ÷ 1000

4 (a) 74.2 × 100
  (b) 74.2 ÷ 100

5 (a) 89.16 × 10
  (b) 89.16 ÷ 10

6 (a) 71.42 × 1000
  (b) 71.42 ÷ 1000

7 (a) 5643 × 10
  (b) 5643 ÷ 10

8 (a) 81 924 × 1000
  (b) 81 924 ÷ 1000

9 (a) 63 057 × 100
  (b) 63 057 ÷ 100

Copy and complete each table.

10 100 centimetres = 1 metre.

	cm	m
(a)	325	
(b)	26.5	
(c)		4.75
(d)		7.4

11 1000 metres = 1 kilometre.

	m	km
(a)	5826	
(b)	741.9	
(c)		1.6
(d)		0.745

12 A class knitted a very long scarf.
It measured 4511 cm.
What was its length in metres?

13 Some cooks baked an enormous
pie. It weighed 1270 kg.
How many grams did it weigh?

keeping skills sharp

Change to the units given in brackets

1 28 cm (mm)   2 46 mm (cm)   3 9.4 m (cm)   4 380 cm (m)

5 4 cm 8 mm (mm)   6 2 m 40 cm (cm)   7 1 km 670 m (m)

8 1 m 510 mm (mm)   9 7800 mm (m).

Squares.

$1 \times 1 = 1$ $2 \times 2 = 4$ $3 \times 3 = 9$ $4 \times 4 = 16$

I expect the next square will have 25 small squares. $5 \times 5 = 25$

To square a number you multiply it by itself. The square of 12 is 144 because $12 \times 12 = 144$.

We can write 12×12 as 12^2.

This is read as 'Twelve squared'. The small 2 in 12^2 is called the **index**. 144 written in index form is 12^2.

Use your calculator if you like.

1 Square these numbers.
   (a) **6**   (b) **9**   (c) **10**   (d) **13**   (e) **15**   (f) **20**

2 Copy and complete this table of squares.

Number	0	1	2	3	4	5	6	7	8	9	10
Square	0	1	4	9					64		

Number	11	12	13	14	15	16	17	18	19	20
Square										

3

A square field has sides 82 m long.
   (a) What is the area of the field?
   (b) What is the perimeter of the field?

82 m

82 m

4 Calculate (i) the area and (ii) the perimeter of squares with sides of:
   (a) **50 cm**   (b) **100 m**   (c) **7 km**   (d) **9 mm**   (e) **28 m**

Squares and square roots (1).

There are 9 square units.
$3 \times 3 = 9$ or $3^2 = 9$
We say 9 is the square of 3
and 3 is the **square root** of 9.

Three squared equals nine.

The square root of 9 is written as $\sqrt{9}$,
so $\sqrt{9} = 3$.

Here is another example:

$5^2 = 5 \times 5 = 25$ 5 squared equals 25.

$\sqrt{25} = 5$ The square root of 25 is 5.

What number multiplied by itself gives 36?

Answer: $6 \times 6 = 36$, so 6 multiplied by itself gives 36.

Write 36 in index form.

Answer: 36 in index form is 6^2.

What is the square root of 36?

Answer: The square root of 36 is 6.

1   Find the square root of

(a) 4   (b) 25   (c) 64   (d) 100

2   Find these.

(a) $\sqrt{16}$ (b) $\sqrt{49}$ (c) $\sqrt{81}$ (d) $\sqrt{1}$

3 A square garden has an area of
   81 square metres.

   (a)   What is the length of each side?
   (b)   What is the perimeter of the
         garden?

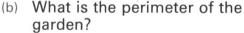

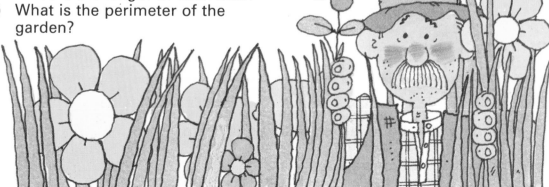

Cubes.

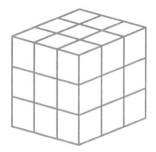

$1 \times 1 \times 1 = 1$ $2 \times 2 \times 2 = 8$ $3 \times 3 \times 3 = 27$

The shapes above are cubes. The numbers show how many small cubes have been used to build them.

The numbers also give the volumes in unit cubes. The base of the cube on the right is 3×3, and the shape is 3 high. $3 \times 3 \times 3 = 27$ unit cubes.

We write $1 \times 1 \times 1$ as 1^3, $2 \times 2 \times 2$ as 2^3, and $3 \times 3 \times 3$ as 3^3.
(This is called the **index form**.)

1^3 is read as 'one cubed', 2^3 as 'two cubed', and 3^3 as 'three cubed'.

You will need a calculator for some of this work.

1   Cube these numbers.
    (a)   **4**   (b)   **5**   (c)   **6**   (d)   **7**   (e)   **10**

2   Use a calculator to find the value of
    (a) 8^3 (b) 9^3 (c) 11^3 (d) 12^3 (e) 20^3

3

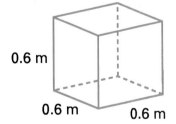

0.6 m   0.6 m   0.6 m

This cube has a volume of
$0.6 \text{ m} \times 0.6 \text{ m} \times 0.6 \text{ m}$ or $(0.6)^3 \text{ m}^3$.

Use your calculator to
   (a)   find the area of the base
   (b)   multiply your answer to (a) by 0.6 m
       to find the volume of the cube.

4   Use the method of question 3 to find $(0.8)^3 \text{ m}^3$.

5   Use a calculator to evaluate
    (a) $(0.4)^3$ (b) $(1.2)^3$ (c) $(2.7)^3$ (d) $(4.5)^3$

The big hike.

1   Raj had £53.72. He bought a rucksack for £25.20 and a sleeping bag for £22.89 before going on a hike.
How much money did he have left?

2   Six hikers took enough water so that they could each drink 1.75 litres of water each day.
How much water did they take for the 2-day hike?

3   The total food bill for the 6 hikers was £51.00. What was each hiker's share of the food cost? Give your answer to the nearest penny.

4   The leader and the 5 hikers carried a total of 61 kg of food and equipment. The leader carried 16 kg and the rest was divided among the other hikers. How much did each carry?

5   The group had a map that used a scale of 1 cm for 2 km.
On the map they found that it was 3.5 cm from the starting point to where they were to have lunch. How far did they have to hike before lunch?

6   After lunch they hiked 9 km before taking a break. If it took them 3 hours, how many km did they average each hour?

7   The exact height of the mountain was 2856.4 m, and the group had climbed exactly 1783.8 m. How far did they still have to climb?

Number problems.

School Sports Day.

1 This year 216 people attended the school sports day.
   This was 39 people more than last year.
   How many people attended sports day last year?

2 The refreshment stall sold 192 packets of crisps at 20p per packet, 79 cans of cola at 55p per can and 48 cups of tea at 30p per cup.
   How much money did the refreshment stall take?

3 (a) The seats were in 12 rows with 14 seats in each row. How many people could be seated?
   (b) How many of the 216 people at the sports could not be seated?

4 The times for the 100-metre sprint were:
   Jones, 16.24 seconds
   Sato, 16.42 seconds
   Weaver, 15.94 seconds
   Morris, 15.09 seconds
   (a) Who had the best time?
   (b) Who had the worst time?

5 Members of the swimming team sold lemonade at the sports day. They sold 92 lemonades for 25p each.
   How much money did they get?

6 The sale of cakes raised £12.65, and the biscuits raised £11.50. The total costs were £8.23.
   How much profit was made?

7   (a) Of the 75 pupils who
        competed in the sports
        $\frac{2}{5}$ were girls.
        How many girls is that?
    (b) How many boys competed?

8   The first- and last-place times in
    the 200-metre sprint were 36.03
    seconds and 39.58 seconds.
    What was the difference in the
    times?

9   The relay team ran the 4 laps in
    the 1600-metre relay in 80, 82.1,
    79.8, and 81.3 seconds.
    What was the total time?

10 In the 100-metre sprint, Morris
    (15.09 seconds) set a new school
    record by 0.18 seconds.
    What was the old record?

11 A year ago, Lucy ran the
    400-metre race in 82.23 seconds.
    This year she improved her time
    by 2.47 seconds.
    What was her time this year?

12 The winner's times for a 5-lap
    race were:
    1st lap 88.2 seconds
    2nd lap 89 seconds
    3rd lap 90.3 seconds
    4th lap 81.7 seconds
    5th lap 90.8 seconds
    (a) What was the total time?
    (b) What was the average time
         for a lap?

Probability.

If you toss a penny it could land or ⬤ uppermost; this is called the **outcome**.

Both outcomes are equally likely.
We say there is an **even chance** it will be a 'head' (or a 'tail').
If you toss a coin 10 times the most likely outcome is 5 heads and 5 tails.
However, you will find many other outcomes, such as 6 heads and 4 tails.

Experiment	Toss a coin.	Throw a dice.	Spin.	Pick a bead without looking.
Possible outcomes	Head or tail	1, 2, 3, 4, 5 or 6 dots	1, 2 or 3	Black bead or red bead
What is the most likely outcome, or are they equally likely?	Equally likely	Equally likely	2 most likely	Black bead most likely

1 Carry out the experiments shown in the table.
Do them at least 10 times.
Record your results.
Discuss them with your teacher.

2 What would be the most likely result if:
  (a) you tossed a coin 20 times?
  (b) you threw a dice 18 times?
  (c) you spun the pointer on the spinner 8 times?
  (d) you picked a bead 14 times, replacing the
      one taken each time?

Probability.

On a dice, the chance of any one number being thrown is one chance in six.
There are six equally likely outcomes.
The probability of each outcome is 1 in 6.
We write this as $\frac{1}{6}$ (any one number is likely to be thrown in one sixth of the throws).

The probability of 4 coming up is $\frac{1}{6}$

$$P(4) = \frac{1}{6}$$

I write this!

We read this as 'the probability of 4 is one sixth or one chance in six'.

$$P(\text{either 2 or 3}) = \frac{1}{6} + \frac{1}{6} = \frac{1}{3}$$

> If something is certain to happen, it has a probability of 1.
> If something is certain **not** to happen, it has a probability of 0.

Find these probabilities when the dice is thrown once.

1 $P(6)$ 2 $P(1)$ 3 $P(5)$ 4 $P(3 \text{ or } 4)$

5 $P(5 \text{ or } 6)$ 6 $P(2, 4 \text{ or } 6)$ 7 $P(\text{odd number})$ 8 $P(\text{prime number})$

9 $P(\text{number greater than 4})$ 10 $P(\text{number less than 4})$

11 $P(2 \text{ and } 3 \text{ at the same time})$ 12 $P(1, 2, 3, 4, 5 \text{ or } 6)$ 13 $P(7)$

keeping skills sharp

Give the highest common factor.

1   12, 18   2   6, 15   3   10, 20   4   9, 12   5   6, 7

Give the lowest common multiple.

6   3, 5   7   2, 5   8   4, 8   9   2, 8   10   3, 7

A   Draw a circle with a radius
of 5 cm.
Draw angles of 45°
from the centre of the
circle.
Label the points
A–H as shown.
Use a pencil as
you may wish to
rub these lines
out later.

B   Join A to B, B to C,
C to D, D to E, E to F,
F to G, G to H
and H to A to form a
regular octagon.

(An 'octagon' has
8 sides.)

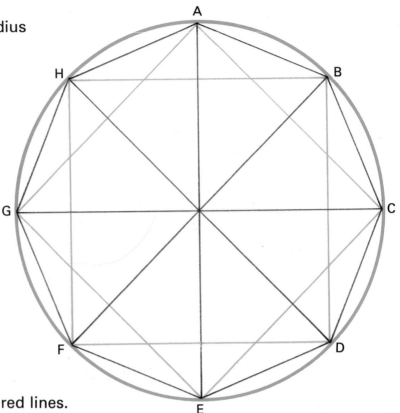

C   Join H to B, B to D,
D to F and F to H with red lines.
What shape have you made?

D   Join A to C, C to E, E to G and G to A with red lines.
What shape have you made?

E   By rubbing out any lines you don't need, and adding any others you want,
you can make several patterns, including these:

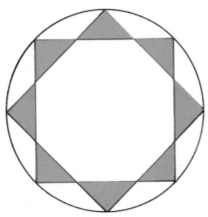

Draw some other patterns based on the regular octagon.
Colour them and make a frieze.

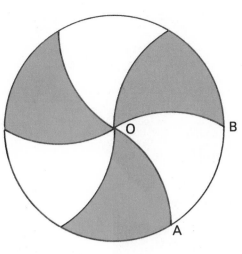

1 (a) Draw a circle with a radius of 3 cm.
        Mark a point on the circumference (A).

   (b) Keep the compasses set at 3 cm.
        With centre A, draw the arc OB.
        With centre B, draw another arc.
        Carry on in this way to get the
        arcs shown.

   (c) Colour your pattern.

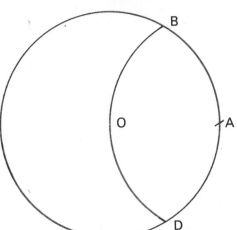

2 Start as before, but continue the arc in
   step (b) to get BOD.
   Carry on exactly as before but making
   the larger arc each time.

   You should then get this pattern.
   Colour it.

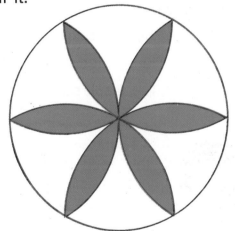

3 See if you can discover how to
   make these patterns.

 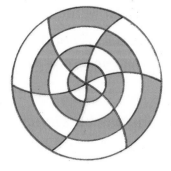

4 Make some patterns of
   your own.
   Colour them.

Introducing algebra.

I am thinking of a number n. When I add 8 to it I get 10. What is the number I am thinking of?

$n + 8 = 10$
Subtract 8 from each side.
$n + 8 - 8 = 10 - 8$
$n = 2$

Write down the equations, then solve them.

1 Add 5 to n. The result equals 9. What does n equal?

2 Add 9 to p. The result equals 20. What does p equal?

3 Add 7 to r. The result equals 13. What does r equal?

4 Add 11 to t. The result equals 19. What does t equal?

If I subtract 5 from n the result equals 9. Find n.

$n - 5 = 9$
Add 5 to each side.
$n - 5 + 5 = 9 + 5$
$n = 14$

5 Subtract 3 from n. The result equals 7. What does n equal?

6 Subtract 8 from f. The result equals 10. What does f equal?

7 Subtract 12 from g. The result equals 1. What does g equal?

8 Subtract 15 from h. The result equals 20. What does h equal?

9 Tom is n years old. In 8 years he will be 20 years old. How old is Tom?

10 Sally is p years old. In 14 years she will be 27 years old. How old is Sally?

11 Fred is 29 years old. In x years he will be 51 years old. Find x.

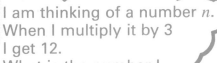

I am thinking of a number n.
When I multiply it by 3
I get 12.
What is the number I
am thinking of?

$n \times 3 = 12$.
Divide both sides
by 3 and they will
be equal. This
will leave n by
itself on the left.

$$\frac{n \times \cancel{3}^{1}}{\cancel{3}_{1}} = \frac{12}{3}$$

$$n = 4$$

Write down the equations, then solve them.

12 Multiply n by 4. The result equals 20. What does n equal?

13 Multiply n by 6. The result equals 42. What does n equal?

14 Multiply p by 3. The result equals 21. What does p equal?

15 Multiply q by 7. The result equals 56. What does q equal?

If I divide n by 2
the result is 16.
Find n.

$$\frac{n}{2} = 16$$

Multiply both sides by 2.

$$\frac{n}{\cancel{2}_{1}} \times \cancel{2}^{1} = 16 \times 2$$

$$n = 32$$

16 Divide n by 5. The result equals 2. What does n equal?

17 Divide n by 2. The result equals 10. What does n equal?

18 Divide p by 6. The result equals 7. What does p equal?

19 Divide r by 3. The result equals 9. What does r equal?

20 Kay's age is x years. Her sister is 3 times that age.
    What is Kay's age if her sister is 15 years old?

21 Tim has saved £x. Beverley has saved only half as much.
    Beverley saved £8. How much has Tim saved?

22 Robin weighs x kg. His sister weighs 15 kg.
    The sister is one fifth of Robin's weight.
    How much does Robin weigh?

Algebra: addition and subtraction.

2 + 2 + 2 + 2 can be written as 2 × 4 (2 multiplied by 4).
Similarly, $a + a + a + a$ can be written as $a \times 4$ (a multiplied by 4).
However it is usual to write the number first and to omit the multiplication sign.
$a + a + a + a$ is therefore **simplified** to $4a$.

Other examples

$b + b + b = 3b$

$2c + 3c = (c + c) + (c + c + c) = 5c$

$4d - 3d = d + d + d + d - d - d - d = d$

Simplify.

1 (a) $e + e + e + e + e$ (b) $f + f + f + f + f + f$ (c) $h + h + h + h + h + h + h$

   (d) $c + c - c$ (e) $d + d + d + d + d - d - d$ (f) $a + a + a + a - a - a - a$

2 (a) $5a + 2a$ (b) $6a + 7a$ (c) $3a + 2a + a$

   (d) $9a - 5a$ (e) $4a - 3a$ (f) $7a - a$

   (g) $7x + 2x - 3x$ (h) $9x - 4x + 3x$ (i) $x + 8x - 2x$

$6x + 3y + 2x + 8y$.
Add $6x$ and $2x$ to find
how many xs there are.
Then add $3y$ and $8y$ to
find the number of ys.
The answer is $8x + 11y$.

It's just as easy with
subtraction.
$7x + 8y - 6x - 3y$
$7x - 6x = x$
$8y - 3y = 5y$
The answer is $x + 5y$.

3 (a) $2x + 3y + 7x + 8y$ (b) $x + 5y + 10x + 2y$

   (c) $5x + 2y + 7y + x$ (d) $15y + 4x + 3y + 9x$

   (e) $x + 5y + 6y + 3x + 5x + y$ (f) $7y + y + x + 8x + 3y + 2x$

   (g) $9x + 6y - 4x - 2y$ (h) $8y - 3y + 7x - 2x$

   (i) $2y + 6x - y - 4x$ (j) $5y + 3x - 2x - 5y$

Algebra problems.

Julia has x stamps. Mark has twice as many as Julia.
Altogether they have 240 stamps.
How many stamps does Julia have?
How many stamps does Mark have?

Mark has $x + x$ or $2x$ stamps.
Altogether they have $2x + x$ stamps. This simplifies to $3x$ stamps.

$3x = 240$. Divide both sides by 3. $\frac{3x}{3} = \frac{240}{3}$ so $x = 80$

Julia has 80 stamps. Mark has 160 stamps.

Always check your answer by putting the values into the problem.

Check: Julia has 80. $80 \times 2 = 160$, so Mark has twice as many.
    $80 + 160 = 240$, so altogether they have 240 stamps.

First write down the equations, then solve the problems.

1   Neil had 28 pence. He was given
    x pence. He then had 50 pence.
    How much was he given?

2   Carol has $2x$ marbles and Andrew
    has $3x$ marbles.
    Together they have 120 marbles.
    Find how many marbles they each
    have.

3

Joanne bought a dress for £x and
a coat for £$3x$.
She spent £44 altogether.
Find the cost of the dress and the
cost of the coat.

4

Ruth baked $6x$ cakes. She ate
x cakes and gave 8 cakes to John.
She then had 2 cakes left.
(a)   How many cakes did she eat?
(b)   How many cakes did she bake?

5   I thought of a number, multiplied it by 5 and then subtracted 2.
    The number I then had was 13.
    What was the number I thought of?

60 seconds (s) = 1 minute (min)
60 minutes = 1 hour (h)
24 hours = 1 day (d)

To change seconds to minutes, divide by 60.
To change minutes to seconds, multiply by 60.

Copy and complete these.

1   (a) 8 minutes = __ seconds   (b) 7 min = __ s   (c) 14 min = __ s

2   (a) 120 seconds = __ minutes   (b) 240 s = __ min   (c) 720 s = __ min

3   (a) To change hours to minutes, _____ by 60.

    (b) To change minutes to hours, _____ by 60.

4   (a) 5 hours = __ minutes   (b) 6 h = __ min   (c) 10 h = __ min

5   (a) 480 minutes = __ hours   (b) 180 min = __ h   (c) 300 min = __ h

6   (a) 3 h 15 min = __ min   (b) 2 h 55 min = __ min   (c) 4 h 6 min = __ min

7   Change to the stated units:

    (a) 42 h = __ d __ h   (b) 117 h = __ d __ h

8   Add.

    (a)   5 h 50 min   (b)   15 min 25 s   (c)   6 d 19 h   (d)   16 h 24 min
         + 2 h 28 min   + 7 min 43 s   + 2 d 18 h   + 9 h 40 min

9   Subtract.

    (a)   7 h 45 min   (b)   10 min 15 s   (c)   5 d 3 h   (d)   10 h 13 min
         − 2 h 28 min   − 5 min 36 s   − 2 d 21 h   − 8 h 50 min

Work with a friend. You will need a calculator!

10   Find out how many hours each of you has been alive.

11   Work out how many minutes of free time you get in one school term.
     (You will have to decide between you what counts as 'free time'.)

More about time.

Classes at one school begin at 8:30. 1 hour and 45 minutes later, break begins. There are several ways to find when break starts. Here are two.

school begins   1 hour later   45 minutes later

school begins   2 hours later   count back 15 minutes

This way is easier for me!

Can you think of another way to find break time?

1   **What time is:**

(a) 30 minutes later than 6:30?

(b) 45 minutes later than 8:45?

(c) 1 hour and 10 minutes later than 9:36?

(d) 1 hour earlier than 5:15?

(e) 1 hour and 15 minutes later than 4:55?

(f) 1 hour and 35 minutes earlier than 4:30?

2 How much time do you have in your school:

(a) from the beginning of school to break?

(b) from the end of break to dinner time?

(c) from the end of dinner time to the next break?

(d) from the end of break to the end of the school day?

(e) How much time do you spend in the classroom:
  (i) during one day?
  (ii) during one week?

3 Jan arrived at the bus stop at 7:55. The bus was due at 8:13. How much time did she have to wait?

4 Terry started on a bike ride at 8:35 a.m. 5 hours and 42 minutes later he completed the ride. What time was that?

'5 Marcia worked 2 hours and 45 minutes one morning and 3 hours and 35 minutes in the afternoon. How long did she work that day?

6 One morning Alex got up at 7:30 after sleeping $9\frac{1}{2}$ hours. What time did he go to bed?

7 A wheelchair racer won a race in 3 hours 4 minutes 56.8 seconds. The racer who came second had a time of 3 hours 5 minutes 2.3 seconds. By how many seconds did the first racer win?

Equations.

I am thinking of a number n. When I subtract 6 from it the answer is 4. What is the number I am thinking of?

Add 6 to each side.
$n - 6 + 6 = 4 + 6$
$n = 10$

Write down the equations then solve them.

1   Add 7 to n. The result equals 9. What does n equal?

2   Add 12 to n. The result equals 20. What does n equal?

3   Add 15 to n. The result equals 31. What does n equal?

4   Subtract 2 from x. The result equals 7. What does x equal?

5   Subtract 10 from x. The result equals 5. What does x equal?

6   Subtract 14 from x. The result equals 19. What does x equal?

When I multiply a number r by 3, the result is 24. What is the number?

$3r = 24$
Divide each side by 3.
$\frac{3r}{3} = \frac{24}{3}$
$r = 8$

7   Multiply r by 2. The result equals 16. What does r equal?

8   Multiply r by 8. The result equals 72. What does r equal?

9   Multiply r by 10. The result equals 70. What does r equal?

10   Divide p by 4. The result equals 6. What does p equal?

11   Divide p by 5. The result equals 45. What does p equal?

12   Divide p by 9. The result equals 81. What does p equal?

Equations and formulae.

Each book costs £8.
What is the cost of 15 books?
Cost = £8 × 15 = £120.

Compare this with:

Each book costs £p.
What is the cost of n books?
Cost = £p × n or £pn.

If the cost is c then $c = pn$.

To solve the following questions it may help you to think of a similar question with numbers replacing the letters. Decide on the operation you need to use (+, −, × or ÷) and then write down the equation.

1   Write down an equation giving the total cost £c, of a book costing £p and two books costing £q each.

   Find c when (a) $p = 6$ and $q = 9$

   (b) $p = 3.45$ and $q = 10$

2   Write down an equation to change n millimetres to t centimetres.

   Also write down an equation to change t centimetres to n millimetres.

   Use your formulae to change (a) 683 mm to centimetres

   (b) 17.4 mm to centimetres

   (c) 1.49 cm to millimetres

   (d) 32 cm to millimetres

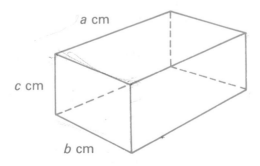

a cm

c cm

b cm

3   The dimensions of a box are a cm, b cm and c m.

   (a) Write down a formula for the surface area (S) in terms of a, b and c.

   (b) Calculate S when $a = 10$, $b = 5$ and $c = 6$.

Think of a number.

1 Think of a number.

Add 7.

Multiply by 2.

Add 6.

Divide by 2.

Subtract the original number.

The answer is 10.

By copying and completing the work shown in the picture you will see that the answer is always 10, no matter what number you think of.

Check that this is true when the number you think of is:

(a) **5**   (b) **11**   (c) **14**   (d) **28**   (e) $1\frac{1}{2}$

2 Let x be the number you think of in each case. Express each of the steps algebraically as you did in question 1.

(a)

Think of a number.
Double it.
Add 15.
Add on the original number.
Divide by 3.
Add 6.
Subtract the original number.
The answer is 11.
Check that the answer is 11
when the starting number is:

(i) **5** (ii) **4** (iii) **3.2** (iv) $1\frac{1}{2}$

(b)

Think of a number.
Multiply it by 3.
Add 32.
Subtract the original number.
Divide by 2.
Subtract 12.
Subtract the original number.
The answer is 4.
Check that the answer is 4
when the starting number is:

(i) **7** (ii) **3** (iii) **2.4** (iv) $\frac{1}{2}$

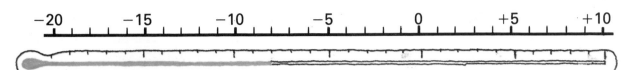

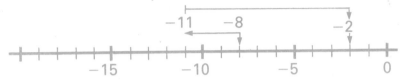

The thermometer shows temperatures in degrees Celsius (°C)
The temperature is −8°C in Moscow.
It falls 3°C. The temperature is then −11°C.

If the temperature rose 9°C it would then be −2°C.
We can show this as   −8 − 3 = −11
                          and −11 + 9 = −2

1   Draw your own number line from −20 to +10.
    Use it to calculate the following:

    (a)   −4 −7   (b)   −6 +5   (c)   0 −8   (d)   +3 −7   (e)   +2 +7

    (f)   +4 −6 −2   (g)   0 +2 −8   (h)   9 −0 −10   (i)   4 +3 −8

Phil had £50 (+50). He spent £20 (−20).
How much did he have left? (+50 −20 = +30)
He had £30 left.
He put the £30 in the bank. He then spent £35.
By how much was his bank account overdrawn?
(+30 −35 = −5). His account was £5 overdrawn.

2   Use the method above to find the amount
    in each account.

    (a)   £20 in the bank. £38 spent.

    (b)   £10 overdrawn. £15 spent.

    (c)   Nothing in the bank. £25 put in. £28 spent.

    (d)   £40 in the bank. £32 spent, then another £9.

    (e)   £200 in the bank. £240 spent. £80 put in the bank.

Imperial and metric units.

You need the following items. They should be in metric and imperial units. Scales for weighing; rulers and tape measures. You also need some bottles and jugs, exercise books, pencils and a local map for question 12.

Estimate first in both the units given in brackets.
Then measure as accurately as you can.

1   Your height (inches, centimetres).

2   Your weight (pounds, kilograms).

3   The area of your hand (square inches, square centimetres).

4   The capacity of the bottles and jugs (pints, litres or millilitres).

5   The perimeter and area of this mathematics book (inches, centimetres, square inches, square centimetres).

6   The lengths of 5 pencils of different lengths (inches, centimetres). Calculate the average length of the pencils.

7   The perimeter of your foot (inches, centimetres).

8   The lengths of the four fingers on your right hand (inches, centimetres). Find the average length (inches, centimetres).

9   The weight of ten exercise books, all the same size (ounces, grams). What is the weight of one exercise book?

10   The width of your shoe (inches, millimetres).

11   The length of your shoe (inches, centimetres).

12   The distance from your home to school (miles or yards, kilometres or metres depending on how far you live from your school)

13   Use a calculator to convert from one unit to another. This will help you to check your answers to questions 1 to 12.

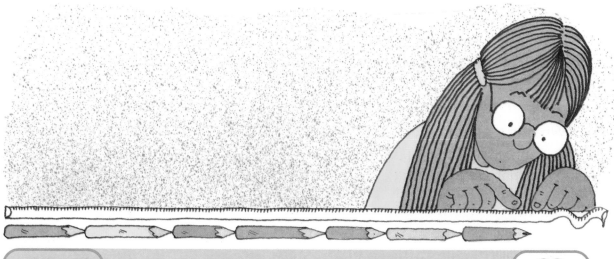

Circles, triangles, hexagons and squares.

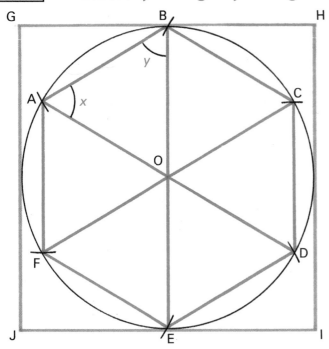

Step 1. Draw a circle with a radius of 4 cm.

Step 2. Mark any point A on the circumference of the circle.

Step 3. With the compasses still set at 4 cm put the point of the compasses at A and mark off point B as shown.

Step 4. Put the point of the compasses on B and mark off C.

Step 5. Continue in this way until you finish back at A. Call the points A, B, C, D, E and F.

Step 6. Join the points in order and you form a regular polygon. This polygon has six sides — it is called a **regular** hexagon. (Regular means all sides are equal and so are the angles.)

1 Join the centre of the circle, O, to A, B, C, D, E and F.
   (a) What are the lengths of the sides of triangle OAB?
   (b) Are all the other triangles the same size and shape as triangle OAB?
   (c) The six angles at O have a total of 360°.
       What is the number of degrees in each angle?
   (d) How many degrees are there in angles x and y?

A triangle with equal sides and equal angles is called an **equilateral triangle**.

2 What is the perimeter of the hexagon ABCDEF?

3 (a) Check that GHIJ in the illustration is a square.
   (b) What are the lengths of its sides?
   (c) What is its perimeter?

4   The diameter of the circle is 8 cm.
    Copy and complete these statements.
    (a) The perimeter of the hexagon is the diameter of the circle
        multiplied by __ .
    (b) The perimeter of the square is the diameter of the circle
        multiplied by __ .
    (c) The circumference of the circle is greater than the perimeter of
        the __ but less than the perimeter of the __.

5   You need a cylinder.
    (a) Place it between two books so that
        the edges of the books are parallel.
        Measure the distance between
        the books. This gives the length of the
        diameter of the cylinder.
    (b) Use string to measure the distance
        round the cylinder (circumference).
    (c) Divide the circumference by the
        diameter if you have a calculator.
        If not, multiply the diameter
        by 2, 3, 4 and 5.
        Which of the four answers is
        nearest to the circumference?

6   Compare your answers to 4(c) and 5(c).
    Discuss them with your teacher.

7   Repeat question 5 with other cylinders.

8   Copy and complete the
    following statement.

    **The circumference of a circle is a
    little more than the
    diameter multiplied by __ .**

9   Look up the Greek letter pi (π)
    in an encylopedia.
    Write some notes so that you
    can tell someone else about it.

Circumference.

This is how to measure the circumference of a circular tin.

A Wrap a strip of paper round the tin.

B Mark the point where the strip has gone round exactly once.

C Open out the strip and measure it up to the mark.

circumference

1 Collect a number of objects that have circles you can measure.
   For example:

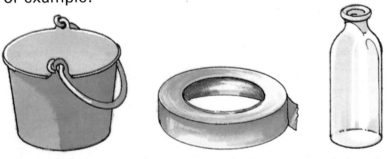 

Measure the circumferences and diameters of the circles.

2 Copy and complete this table. Record your results from question 1 on it.
   Measure other round objects and include them in the table.

Object	Circumference	Diameter

3 Copy and complete this sentence.
   The circumference is a little more than ___ times the diameter.

Find $\frac{2}{5}$ of 20.
First find $\frac{1}{5}$ of 20, which is 4.
Multiply this by 2 to find $\frac{2}{5}$.
The answer is 8.

Here is another way.

$\frac{2}{5}$ of 20 means the same as

$\frac{2}{5} \times 20$ which can be rewritten as $\frac{2 \times 20}{5}$

Divide numerator and denominator by 5.

$\frac{2 \times \overset{4}{20}}{\underset{1}{5}} = \frac{8}{1} = 8$

You can do it like this:

$\frac{2}{\underset{1}{5}} \times \overset{4}{20} = 8$

We call this **cancelling**.

1	$\frac{3}{4}$ of 28	2	$\frac{2}{3}$ of 18	3	$\frac{3}{5}$ of 60	4	$\frac{2}{3}$ of 90
5	$\frac{5}{6}$ of 24	6	$\frac{3}{8}$ of 48	7	$\frac{5}{4}$ of 20	8	$\frac{3}{2}$ of 30
9	$\frac{5}{7}$ of 35	10	$\frac{3}{4}$ of 24p	11	$\frac{1}{2}$ of 56p	12	$\frac{2}{3}$ of 81p
13	$\frac{3}{5}$ of 75p	14	$\frac{2}{3}$ of £15	15	$\frac{3}{8}$ of 32p	16	$\frac{3}{10}$ of £40

17 A baker made 100 dozen biscuits. She had sold $\frac{3}{5}$ of them before noon. How many dozen were sold?

18 The baker's recipe for angel cake makes enough mixture for 30 cakes. Today she used only $\frac{2}{3}$ of the recipe. How many cakes did that make?

19 One recipe called for $\frac{3}{4}$ tablespoon of salt. The baker doubled the recipe. How much salt was used?

20 Left-over baked items are sold the next day at $\frac{2}{5}$ off the full price. If the full price of 12 doughnuts is £2.00, what is the sale price?

Conversion graph for UK pounds (£) and USA dollars ($)

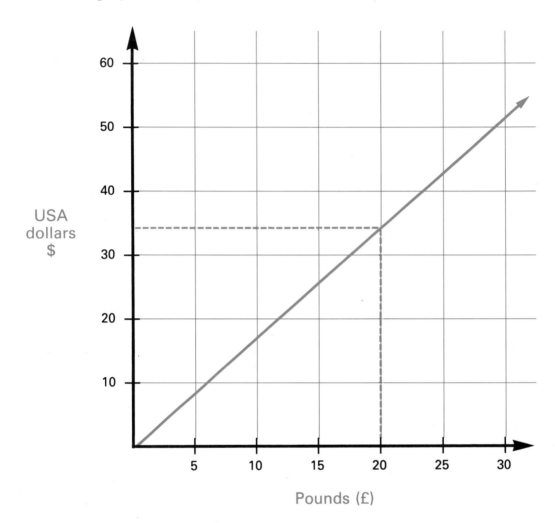

The graph shows that £20 is approximately equal to $34.50.

1 Change to USA dollars.

   (a) £5   (b) £17   (c) £23   (d) £28.50

2 Change to pounds.

   (a) $20   (b) $43   (c) $48   (d) $8.50

3 Take £1 = $1.732. Use a calculator to find the answers to
   questions 1 and 2. Round your answers to two decimal places.

Use a calculator.

1 £1 = 180.29 Spanish pesetas.
   What is the value in pesetas of:

   (a) £5   (b) £10
   (c) £16   (d) £19.50

2 Plot a conversion graph for
   Spanish pesetas and pounds.
   Use a scale of 1 cm to £2.50 on
   the horizontal axis and 1 cm to
   500 pesetas on the vertical axis.

3 Use your graph to change these
   amounts to pesetas.

   (a) £3   (b) £11

   (c) £12.50   (d) £23.50

4 Use a calculator to find the
   answers to question 3 correct
   to two decimal places.

5 Use your graph to change these
   amounts to pounds.

   (a) 720 pesetas   (b) 2000 pesetas

   (c) 3400 pesetas   (d) 4150 pesetas

6 Use a calculator to find the
   answers to question 5 correct
   to two decimal places.

Discussion points

What point will all conversion graphs for currency pass through?

Where can you see currency rates displayed?

Why do they change from day to day?

Why are all money conversion graphs straight line graphs?

What conversion graphs could you draw that are not for money?

The Target Number Game.

.47 is another way of writing 0.47
We usually write 0.47 but
either can be used.

Which is closer to the target number, 50?

1 (a) $\boxed{5}\boxed{2}$ + $\boxed{7}\boxed{6}$ − $\boxed{8}\boxed{4}$

   (b) $\boxed{7}\boxed{8}$ + $\boxed{4}\boxed{5}$ − $\boxed{2}\boxed{6}$

2 (a) $\boxed{9}\boxed{3}$ + $\boxed{4}\boxed{0}$ − $\boxed{6}\boxed{8}$

   (b) $\boxed{7}\boxed{8}$ + $\boxed{6}\boxed{9}$ − $\boxed{4}\boxed{3}$

Play the game.

A Prepare a card for each of the digits
(0, 1, 2, 3, 4, 5, 6, 7, 8 and 9).

B Each player makes a table like this
on a piece of paper:

   $\square\square$ + $\square\square$ − $\square\square$

C Choose a leader. The leader
shuffles the cards and takes one
card at a time. As each card is
taken write the digit somewhere
in your table.

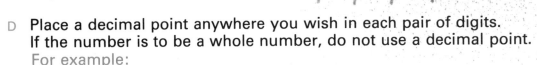

D Place a decimal point anywhere you wish in each pair of digits.
If the number is to be a whole number, do not use a decimal point.
For example:

John's table:

$\boxed{6}\boxed{0}$ + $\boxed{4}\boxed{7}$ − $\boxed{6}\boxed{3}$

Karen's table:

$\boxed{4}\boxed{6}$ + $\boxed{3}\boxed{6}$ − $\boxed{0}\boxed{7}$

E The player closest to the target number, 50, wins the game.
Who came closer, John or Karen?

F Play the game with other target numbers.

A Throwing Game.

How to play.
Mark out a long straight line
longer than you expect anyone
in your class to be able to throw a ball.
This could be done with a long piece of string.
You might use one of the lines on a playing field.
Mark a point A at one end of the line and B at the other end.

Measuring and scoring.
The aim of the game is to throw a ball as far as possible in the direction of B.
The player must throw a ball from A.
Suppose the ball lands at point P.

Measure the line P to C at right angles to AB.
Measure AC.
Subtract PC from AC, that is 30 m − 1.5 m = 28.5 m.
So the score for the throw is 28.5.

1   Work with four others and make a record of your throws. Have five throws
     each.
     Make a list of the best throw made by each person in your group, with the
     greatest distance first and the name of each person beside each throw.

2   Make a bar graph of the greatest distances thrown by ten pupils.

Graphs.

Think about standing still then jumping straight up as high as you can. The distance that you jump beyond your normal reach is your vertical jump. First guess what it would be. Then follow these steps to measure it.

Step 1.
Put a blob of paint on your middle finger. While standing *flat-footed*, mark as high as you can reach on a paper strip that is taped to the wall. Measure the height of your mark to the nearest centimetre. Convert the height to metres.

Step 2.
From a standing position, jump to see how high you can mark on the same paper. Measure the distance to the nearest centimetre and convert it to metres.

Step 3.
Subtract to find your vertical jump in metres. Rounds your answer to two places of decimals.

Step 4.
When all your classmates have measured their vertical jumps, list them on the board.

Step 5.
Find the number of pupils in each of the 0.1 m intervals. Show the results on a grid like this:

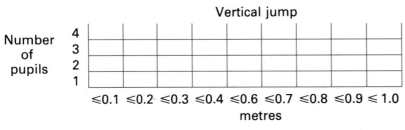

List some facts shown by your graph.

Range, mode and median.

Andy and Pardeep found the height of fifty-three people in their school. They made this chart showing tallies and frequencies.

Height in cm	Tallies	Frequency
$h < 120$	ЦНТ I	6
$120 \leqslant h < 130$	ЦНТ IIII	9
$130 \leqslant h < 140$	ЦНТ ЦНТ ЦНТ	15
$140 \leqslant h < 150$	ЦНТ ЦНТ II	12
$150 \leqslant h < 160$	ЦНТ III	8
$160 \leqslant h$	III	3
h is the height of a pupil	Total	53

$<$ is less than $>$ is greater than

$\geqslant$ is greater than or equal to $\leqslant$ is less than or equal to

The **range** is the difference between the greatest and least height. If the greatest was 168 cm and the least 116 cm the range is 52 cm. (This cannot be found from the table.).

The **mode** is the most frequent value so this is the $130 \leqslant h < 140$ group.

The **median** is the value in the middle when all are placed in order. In the example above it is the value for the 27th pupil (because this is the middle number of the fifty-three pupils). Counting from the shortest (or tallest) we find the 27th pupil is in the $130 \leqslant h < 140$ group. The median value is more than 130 but less than 140.

1   Plan a survey of the heights of pupils in your class. Do this for intervals of 5 cm, instead of the 10 cm intervals used above.

    Find the shortest and tallest pupils and select your extreme values so as to include these. For example if 118 cm and 154 cm you would start at 115 cm and finish at 155 cm. Find the mode and the median.

2   Plan a similar survey but for the weights of pupils.

    Find the range, the mode and the median.

Activity 1

Range, mode, median and mean.

Here are the marks out of 10 that
21 pupils obtained in a mathematics
test.

10 9 9 8 8 8 7 7 6 6
6 5 5 5 5 4 4 3 2 2 0

The same group then took a
geography test.

The marks out of 10 were:

9 9 9 8 8 8 8 7 7 7
6 6 6 6 6 5 5 4 4 3 0

1   What is the range of:

   (a)   the mathematics marks?   (b) the geography marks?

2   What is the mode of:

   (a)   the mathematics marks?   (b)   the geography marks?

3   What is the median of:

   (a)   the mathematics marks?   (b)   the geography marks?

4   Use a calculator to find the total of the marks and the average (or mean) mark for:

   (a)   mathematics   (b) geography

   Give your answers correct to 1 decimal place.

5   Find the difference between:

   (a)   the two ranges (b) the two modes (c) the two medians
   (d)   the two averages

6   In order of size, with the greatest first, write the mode, median and mean for:

   (a)   mathematics   (b) geography

7   Draw a tally and frequency chart for both sets of marks.

Activity 2.

Range, mode, median and mean.

The number of runs scored by three batsmen in one month were:

Bill Bloggs	45	11	0	52	16		
Ben Bradman	13	7	10	29	48	63	4
Harry Hammond	15	3	102	78	9	15	27

1 For each batsman find:

   (a) the range   (b) the median.

2 Each batsman was 'out' in every innings. Using a calculator work out the mean score for each batsman. (This is called their 'batting average'.) Give your answers to the nearest whole number.

3 If Bill Bloggs had one more innings, what would he need to score to make his batting average 32?

4 If Ben Bradman had been 'not out' in one of his innings, the number of innings is counted as 6 not 7. What would his batting average have then been?

5 In the following month Bill Bloggs had 4 innings and was 'out' in all of them. His average score for the two months was 20. Find:

   (a) his total score for the 9 innings

   (b) his average score for the 4 innings in the second month.

Bilateral and rotational symmetry.

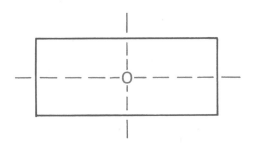

The red lines show the axes of mirror or **bilateral symmetry**.

O is the centre of rotational symmetry.

The rectangle has rotational symmetry of order 2. (If you traced the rectangle it could be fitted on to the original rectangle in 2 ways. These can be found by rotating the tracing around O, but *without turning it over*.)

1   Trace or copy each shape below.
   (i)   Mark the axes of bilateral symmetry, if any.
   (ii) Mark the centre of rotational symmetry, if any.
   (iii) State the order of rotational symmetry.

(a) 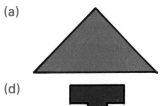   (b)   (c)

(d)    (e)   (f)

This cuboid has three **planes of symmetry**.

   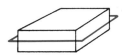   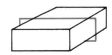

2   How many planes of symmetry do these solids have?

(a)    (b)   (c) 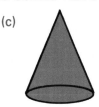   (d)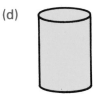

a square-based pyramid   a cube   a cone   a cylinder

3   Draw some other solid shapes and say how many planes of symmetry they have.

In this example the red lines are lines of bilateral symmetry.

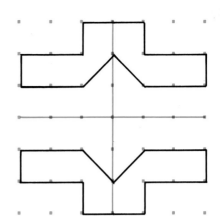

Copy each of these shapes on to dotted paper. You can use graph paper if you prefer.

Complete each shape so that it is symmetrical about both red lines.

1
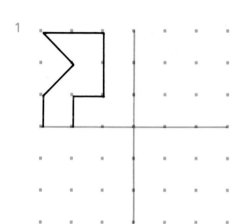

2
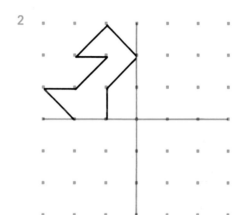

3
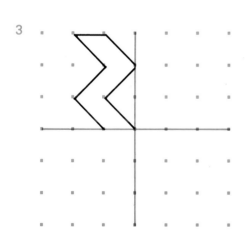

4
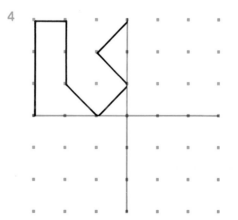

This is an example of rotation about the centre dot:

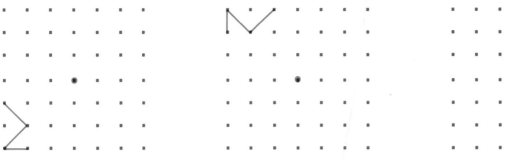

start   after $\frac{1}{4}$ turn   after $\frac{1}{2}$ turn from start

You need dotted or squared paper. Draw the shapes as they will be:
(a) after $\frac{1}{4}$ turn   (b) after $\frac{1}{2}$ turn

1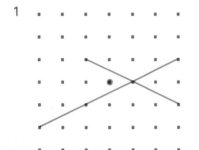

2

3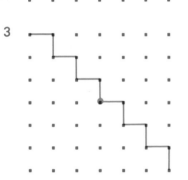

4

keeping skills sharp

1 Round to the nearest 10 and then to the nearest 100.

  (a) 387   (b) 804   (c) 666   (d) 1383
  (e) 2725   (f) 4002   (g) 7996   (h) 10 483

2 Round to the nearest 100 and then to the nearest 1000.

  (a) 2496   (b) 5967   (c) 3961   (d) 8109
  (e) 9950   (f) 10 072 (g) 954   (h) 436

Patterns and sequences.

Sticks and squares.

Small sticks have been used to make the squares A, B, C and D.

A   B   C    D

1 How many sticks have been used to make
  (a) A?   (b) B?   (c) C?   (d) D?

  The lengths of the sides, taking one stick
  as the unit of length, are

  A 1 unit, B 2 units, C 3 units, D 4 units.

2 How many sticks would be needed to make
  (a) E, a square with sides of length 5 units?
  (b) F, a square with sides of length 6 units?

The formula for finding the number of sticks needed is $n = 2u(u + 1)$
where n is the total number of sticks and u is the number of sticks forming
one side of the big square.
In square C above, $u = 3$ so $n = 2 \times 3 \times (3 + 1) = 2 \times 3 \times 4 = 24$

---

3 Use the formula to check your results in questions 1 and 2.

4 Complete the sequence up to $u = 10$.

$u = 1$	2	3	4	5	6	7	8	9	10
A	B	C	D	E	F	G	H	I	J
$n = 4$	—	24	—	—	—	—	—	—	—

5 Try these puzzles. Starting with 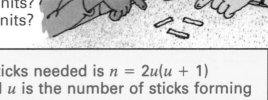 each time:

  (a) take away two sticks so as to leave two squares,
  (b) move four sticks so as to make three squares.

How many pieces?

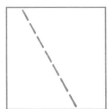

Start with a square of any size.
One line divides it into two pieces.

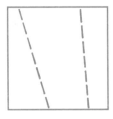 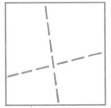

If there are two lines
then the number of pieces
is either three or four.

1   Copy and complete this table.

Number of lines	Smallest number of pieces	Greatest number of pieces
1	2	2
2	3	4
3		
4		
5		

2   If n is the number of lines what is the formula for the smallest number of pieces?

3   The greatest number of pieces is given by the formula

$\frac{1}{2}(n^2 + n + 2)$.

For example, when $n = 2$ this gives

$\frac{1}{2}(2^2 + 2 + 2) = \frac{1}{2}(4 + 2 + 2) = \frac{1}{2}(8) = 4$

Check your answers to question 1 by using the formula.

4   Continue the number of lines up to 10.
Check your answers by using the formula.

Crossings.

Suppose you have 4 sticks, you can have them crossing in various formations.

0 crossing   1 crossing   3 crossings   4 crossings   6 crossings

1   Draw the sticks with: (a) **2 crossings**   (b) **5 crossings**

    (c) **Is it possible to have more than 6 crossings?**

2   Suppose you have 4 sticks but are only allowed to have them laid in two directions. This means there are two sets of parallel lines. With four sticks the number of crossings can be 0 (||||), 1 (||¥), 2 (Ж|), 3 (Ж†) or 4 (#).

    Draw all the possible numbers of ways if you have 5 sticks.

3   The smallest number of sticks needed to make 1 crossing is 2 sticks. If the sticks can be placed in any direction find the smallest number of sticks needed to make:

    (a) **2 crossings**   (b) **3 crossings**   (c) **4 crossings**

4   Copy and complete the table below. Write your answers to question 3 on it.

Number of crossings	Smallest number of sticks needed
1	
2	
3	
4	

Continue the table up to 12 crossings.

The Fibonacci sequence.

1   1   2   3   5   8   13   21   ....

This sequence of numbers goes on for ever.

Each number is obtained by adding the two previous numbers.

These numbers form the Fibonacci sequence, named after the great mathematician, Leonardo Fibonacci.

Fibonacci set the following problem in one of his books:
'Let us suppose that a pair of rabbits are not old enough to breed one month after their birth but in their second month they will have two babies and continue to have two more babies every month after that.
The babies in turn will have two babies when they are in their second month.
If none of the rabbits dies what will the total number be each month?'

Month

1   A 🐰🐰   The first pair A are born.

2   A 🐰🐰   A are too young to have babies.

3   A 🐰🐰 B 🐰🐰   A have babies B.

4   A 🐰🐰 B 🐰🐰 C 🐰🐰   A have babies C.
                                B are too young to have babies.

5   🐰🐰 🐰🐰 🐰🐰 🐰🐰 🐰🐰   A have babies D. B have babies E.
    A   B   C   D   E   C are too young to have babies.

1   Draw the rabbits for the next month. How many pairs are there?

2   The breeding of the rabbits follows the Fibonacci sequence.
    Continue the sequence at the top of the page until there are 20 numbers in the sequence.

Make sure you've completed page 52, because this investigation should produce a pattern from Fibonacci's sequence.

1   1   2   3   5   8   13   21   ....

1   (a)   Choose any one of the Fibonacci numbers and square it.

If we chose 8 then $8^2 = 64$.

Now find the product of the two Fibonacci numbers on either side of your number.

With our example these would be 5 and 13. $5 \times 13 = 65$.

The difference between 65 and 64 is 1.

What was the difference for the number you used?

(b)   Test at least five other numbers in the same way.
What were the differences?

2

$$1^2 = 1 \times 1 = 1$$
$$1^2 + 1^2 = 1 \times 2 = 2$$
$$1^2 + 1^2 + 2^2 = 2 \times 3 = 6$$
$$1^2 + 1^2 + 2^2 + 3^2 = 3 \times 5 = 15$$
$$1^2 + 1^2 + 2^2 + 3^2 + 5^2 =$$
$$1^2 + 1^2 + 2^2 + 3^2 + 5^2 + 8^2 =$$
$$1^2 + 1^2 + 2^2 + 3^2 + 5^2 + 8^2 + 13^2 =$$

Above is a number pattern formed by adding the squares of Fibonacci numbers.

(a)   Complete the last three lines **without** squaring and adding.

(b)   Check your answer to (a) by squaring and adding.

(c)   Write down the next two lines of the pattern.

Investigating the calendar for patterns.

In this example the total of the four numbers inside the rectangle is 56. This can be found by multiplying the number in the top left-hand corner (10) by 4 and then adding 16.
$(10 \times 4) + 16 = 56.$

1   Check that the rule in the example works for these rectangles:

(a)
14	15
21	22

(b)
12	13
19	20

(c)
23	24
30	31

2   Check that it works for at least five other rectangles.

3   (a)
x	$x+1$
$x+7$	$x+8$

Check that this rectangle can represent **all** the rectangles on the calendar.
Discuss your answer with your teacher.

(b)   Use your results from (a) to show **why** the rule in the example works.

4
19	20
26	27

Multiply diagonally as shown.
$19 \times 27 = 513$ $20 \times 26 = 520$
There is a difference of 7.

(a)   Try other rectangles in the same way.

(b)   What do you notice about the differences?

November

Sun	Mon	Tue	Wed	Thur	Fri	Sat
					1	2
3	4	5	6	7	8	9
10	11	12	13	14	15	16
17	18	19	20	21	22	23
24	25	26	27	28	29	30

1 (a) Find the total of the six numbers inside the rectangle.

   (b) The total can also be found by multiplying the number in the top left-hand corner by 6 and then adding on a certain number. Find the number that is to be added.

2 (a)
19	20	21
26	27	28

Check that the rule found in question 1(b) also works for this rectangle.

   (b) Check the rule for other rectangles containing six numbers.

3
11	12
18	19
25	26

   (a) Investigate this rectangle in the same way as you did for questions 1 and 2. What is the rule now?

   (b) Check whether the rule works for other rectangles with three rows and two numbers in each row.

Use algebra, as in question 3 on page 54, to prove that the rules always work for rectangles:

(a) with two rows and three numbers in each row;

(b) with three rows and two numbers in each row.

The Survey File

The SURVEY file contains the records of 30 people on a consumer survey. Each record tells us the name, age, height, home town, car registration number and car colour of one of the people on the list. These are called the **field names**.

The first record looks like this:

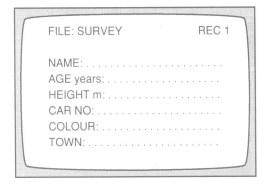

```
FILE: SURVEY              REC 1

NAME: . . . . . . . . . . . . . . . . . . . . .
AGE years: . . . . . . . . . . . . . . . . .
HEIGHT m: . . . . . . . . . . . . . . . . .
CAR NO: . . . . . . . . . . . . . . . . . . .
COLOUR: . . . . . . . . . . . . . . . . . .
TOWN: . . . . . . . . . . . . . . . . . . . .
```

Now use the SURVEY file on the computer. Choose to display the records. Look at the first record – it should be HAROLD BROWN.

1   Now go to the second record.
    Write down all of the details given.

2   Now move on to the sixth record.

    (a) How tall is Felicity?

    (b) What is the colour of her car?

    (c) In which town does she live?

3   Move on carefully through the records until you find HUGH FORT.

    (a) How old is he?

    (b) Give his car registration number.

    (c) What is his home town?

4   Again move through the records carefully until you find a lady from LEEDS.

    (a) What is her name?

    (b) How old is she?

    (c) Describe her car.

Sorting into order.

1   Sort these numbers in order from the largest to the smallest.

| 15 | 31 | 23 | 53 | 7 | 16 |

2   Sort these numbers in order from the smallest to the largest.

| 2.4 | 6.6 | 1.7 | 1.4 | 3.1 | 5.2 |

3   Put these towns into alphabetical order.

| SWINDON | LEEDS | YORK | LONDON | OXFORD |

4   Put these colours into alphabetical order.

| WHITE | GREEN | BLUE | YELLOW | BLACK |

5   (a)   Sort these people in order of age.

| JAMES 15 | SARAH 18 | LUKE 13 | BRENDA 16 | BRUCE 19 |

   (b)   Who is the oldest?

   (c)   Who is the youngest?

6   Now use the SURVEY file on the computer.

   (a)   Choose to sort the records by age. How old is the youngest person?

   (b)   Choose to sort the records by towns. Which are the first 3 alphabetically?

   (c)   Choose to sort the records by names. Give all the surnames between J and Q.

   (d)   Sort by height. Write down the names of the 3 tallest people.

   (e)   Sort by car colour. Give the registration number of all green cars.

   (f)   Sort by age. Name the woman who is a year older than Steve Adnam.

Searching a database.

1 Search through this group.

   (a) How many girls are there?
   (b) How many names contain
        only two vowels?
   (c) How many names, alphabetically,
        come before L?

2 Search through these records.

JAMES	SARAH	LUKE	BRENDA	BRUCE
15	18	13	16	19

FRANK	RUTH	LINDA	SIMON	MARTIN
12	20	15	11	17

   (a) How many are girls?
   (b) How many are younger than 18?
   (c) How many boys are older than 15?

Now use the SURVEY file on the computer.
To find out how many of the people own white cars we:

(select) | SEARCH |

(select) | CAR COLOUR |

(select) | IS THE SAME AS | (type) WHITE

Try this. You should find that there are 4 white cars.

3 Now start a new search with all of the records.
   Each time you search make sure you are using all of the records.

   (a) How many yellow cars are there?
   (b) How many people come from London?

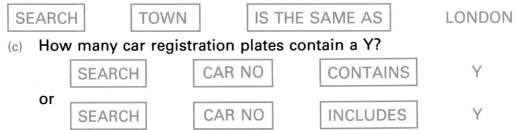

   (c) How many car registration plates contain a Y?

More about multiplication and division.

Method 1
$200 \times 60 = 200 \times 6 \times 10 = (200 \times 6) \times 10 = 1200 \times 10 = 12\,000$

Method 2
Multiply 2 by 6. That's 12.

There are three 0s in 200×60 so there will be three 0s in the answer.

So $200 \times 60 = 12\,000$

Discuss with your teacher why this method works.

1   Multiply 400 by 80 using both the methods given above.
    Check by using a calculator.

2   Use the three ways in question 1 to do these multiplications.

    (a) 90×600 (b) 50×500 (c) 700×60 (d) 400×300

3   What is the total cost of:

    (a)   20 motor-cycles costing £800 each?

    (b)   300 sheep costing £70 each?

$$\frac{800}{20} = \frac{\overset{4}{\cancel{8}} \times 10 \times \overset{1}{\cancel{10}}}{\underset{1}{\cancel{2}} \times \underset{1}{\cancel{10}}} = \frac{40}{1} = 40$$

Divide the 8 by the 2. That's 4.

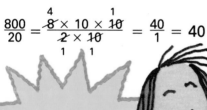

Discuss with your teacher why this method for division works.

Cross off one 0 in 800 and one 0 in 20.
That is the same as dividing them each by 10.

There's one 0 left in the 'top' (numerator).
Therefore $\frac{800}{20} = 40$

4   Use the method to divide 1000 by 50.
    Check your answer by using a calculator.

5   Complete this calculation: $\dfrac{9000}{200} = \dfrac{90 \times }{2 \times } \dfrac{\times }{\times } = \text{--} \text{--} = $

    Simplify: (a) $\dfrac{5000}{200}$ (b) $\dfrac{6000}{400}$ (c) $\dfrac{30}{900}$ (d) $\dfrac{20}{700}$

Ordered pairs and functions.

The sum of two numbers is 12.

This could be written as △ + □ = 12

If we write △3, then we must write □9 to make the sum 12.

If we write △13, then we must write □−1 .

1 **What number must be written in the square?**

(a) △5 (b) △11 (c) △0 (d) △−2 (e) △20

2 **What number must be written in the triangle?**

(a) □8 (b) □−3 (c) □16 (d) □−2 (e) □100

3 The sum of two numbers is 6.
The answers are to be positive whole numbers (0, 1, 2, 3, ...)

□ + △ = 6.

(a) How many possible values can be written in the box?

(b) Write down each pair of values that satisfy the equation.

For example (□2 , △4).

These are called **ordered pairs**.

4 (a) Write down an equation, using a □ and a △, to show 'the difference of two numbers is 5'.

(b) Copy and complete this table, so as to satisfy (a).

□	2	1		−1		−3	4	
△			0		2			−5

5 The product of two numbers is 32.

(a) Write an equation, using □ and △, to represent this.

(b) □ and △ are positive whole numbers.

Find all the possible ordered pairs that satisfy the equation in (a).

A function game.

△	0	1	2	3	4	5
☐	3	5	7	9	11	13

For each value of △ there is only one value of ☐.

Such sets of ordered pairs are called a **function**.

My rule is:
Multiply the number
by 2 and then add 3.

△ × 2 + 3 = ☐

Brian has decided on a rule to change each number he is given. His friends have to find the rule.

1   Check that the values given in the table at the top of this page satisfy Brian's rule.

2   What would Brian give as the value of ☐ if his friends said △ was:

(a) **7?**   (b) **10?**   (c) **1.2?**   (d) **−1?**

3   Brian said ☐ was 21. What number had he been given?

4   Find the rule for the values given below.

(a)

△	−1	0	1	2	3	4	5
☐	−4	−1	2	5	8	11	14

(b)

△	2	5	0	7	−1	10	−5
☐	11	23	3	31	−1	43	−17

Squares and square roots (2).

$2.1 \times 2.1 = 2.1^2 = 4.41$ $\sqrt{4.41} = \sqrt{2.1 \times 2.1} = 2.1$

$2.2^2 = 4.84$ $2.3^2 = 5.29$ $2.4^2 = 5.76$ $2.5^2 = 6.25$

So $\sqrt{5}$ must be somewhere between 2.2 and 2.3

It is nearer to 2.2 than to 2.3 so we will try 2.23^2, 2.24^2 and 2.25^2.

Use your calculator to check: $2.23^2 = 4.9729$, $2.24^2 = 5.0176$, $2.25^2 = 5.0625$,

So $\sqrt{5} \approx 2.24$ because this is the nearest of the values tried.

Use a calculator to work out the following.

1. Square (a) 17   (b) 1.9   (c) 3.8   (d) 4.2   (e) 5.7

   (f) 6.15   (g) 7.89   (h) 12.6   (i) 17.4   (j) 23.4

2. Square 6.39 giving your answer correct to

   (a) the nearest whole number

   (b) one place of decimals

   (c) two places of decimals

3. (a) Square 1.3, 1.4, 1.5, 1.6, 1.7, 1.8, 1.9 and 2.0.

   (b) Using the method given at the top of this page find, to 2 places of decimals, the square roots of (i) 1.8 (ii) 2.1 and (iii) 3.7.

4. A square park has an area of 1.78 square kilometres.

   Calculate (a) the length of a side in (i) kilometres   (ii) metres

   (b) its perimeter in metres

5.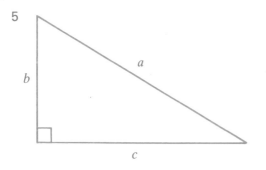

The rule of Pythagoras says that for any right-angled triangle the lengths of the sides are related by the formula

$a^2 = b^2 + c^2$.

a, b and c are the lengths of the sides shown in the diagram.
Calculate a if $b = 4$ and $c = 7$.

Give the answer correct to 2 places of decimals.